AF454317

Introduction

With romance and history in her blood, Paris shows her tender side as never before. Only Paris offers the inimitable stage that can still turn every photo into a film. The city is peerless in its beauty and allure in its architectural splendor, wealth of churches, palaces, parks, and grand boulevards.

Add to that a long, rich, and influential history, and this coveted capital is art in its purest form. From the Eiffel Tower and the Louvre to Montmartre and Saint-Germain-des-Pres, the traces of painters and photographers and echoes of actors and movie directors can be found all over the city.

This sumptuously illustrated book celebrates its glory on the Grands Boulevards and Champs Elysées. It captures its cultural heartbeat in the artists' quarter of Montmartre and the Quartier Latin on the Left Bank.

Lively areas overflowing with art and fashion, as well as lesser-known impressions of the city's banlieues, are all captured with a present-day attention to detail.

There is hardly any corner in Paris where you are not confronted with beauty and decor: it is layered with architectural history and culture. At every turn and corner, it has magnificently decorated buildings of a royal, religious, and secular purpose. Ancient, Gothic, Renaissance, baroque, and modern architecture meld together in a city laid out upon the banks of the Seine.

This is the perfect book for those who have been captured by the romance and beauty of Paris.

Spectacular Paris celebrates all that shines in the beautiful City of Light as an outstanding gift or souvenir in a new Hardback copy.

City Scape Paris

Paris cityscape taken from Montmartre

Parisian Cafe

Arc de Triomphe

Champs-élysées

Champs-élysées

Beautiful sunset over Eiffel Tower

Eiffel Tower in the evening

Sainte Chapelle

The Louvre

The Louvre

Notre dame

Notre Dame

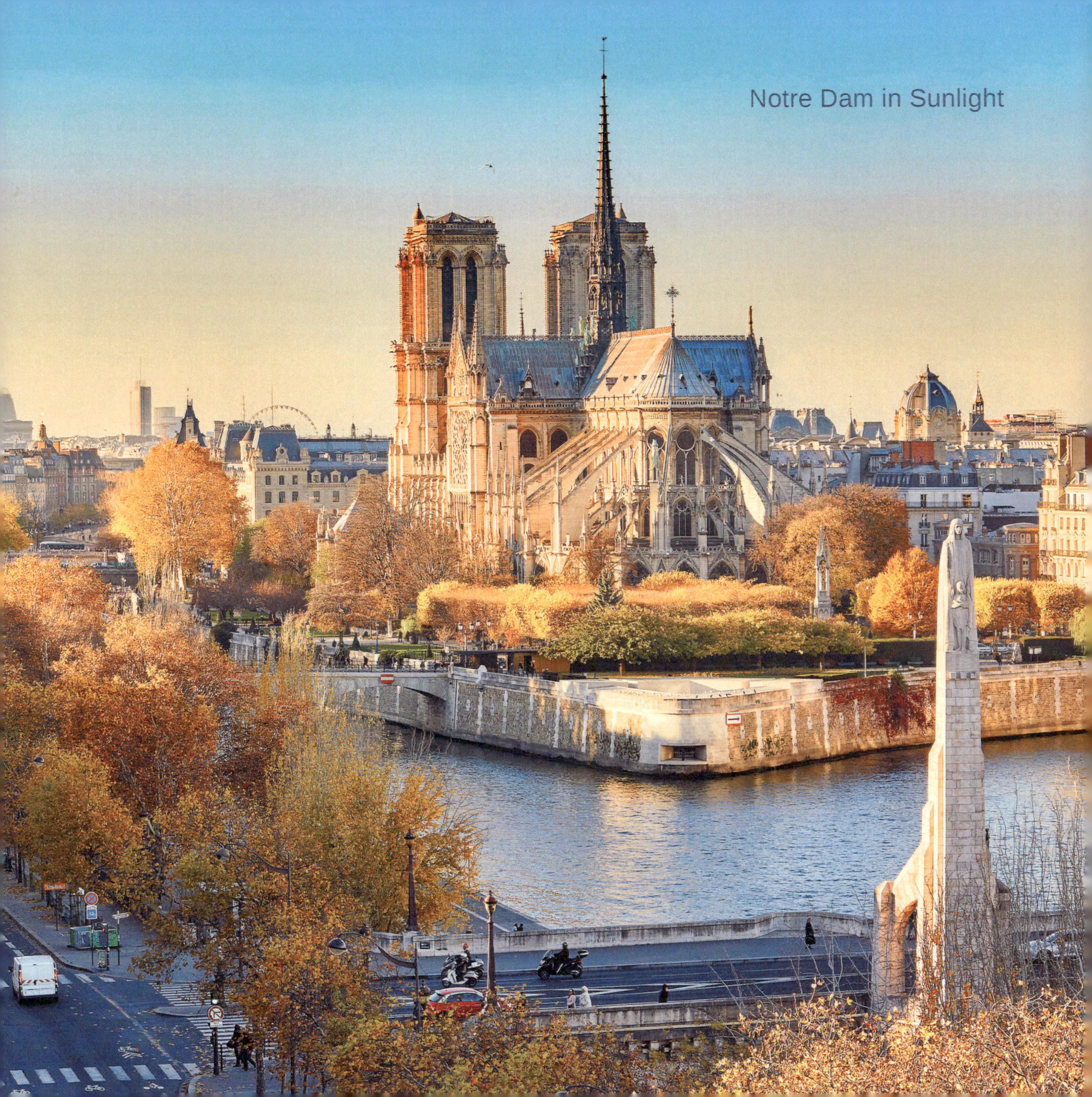
Notre Dam in Sunlight

Château de Versailles

Versailles Garden

Château de Versailles

Versailles Garden

Sacré-Coeur Basilica

Sacré-Coeur Basilica

Sacré-Coeur Basilica

LE CONSULAT
LA BONNE FRANQUETTE
RESTAURANT LE CONSULAT
CAFÉ

Montmartre

Montmartre Stairway

Palais Garnier

Stairway inside the Palais Garnier, opera house in Paris

Musée d'Orsay

Musée d'Orsay

Champ de Mars

Jardin des Tuileries

Galeries Lafayette

Galeries Lafayette

Parc des Buttes-Chaumont

Parc des Buttes-Chaumont

Panthéon

Panthéon

Saint-Germain-des-Près

Saint-Germain-des-Prés

Saint-Germain-des-Près

Moulin Rouge

Mount Etna
AL
DU
ULIN RO
OUGE
Féer

Palais du Luxembourg

Musée Rodin

Disneyland Paris

Disneyland Paris

Catacombs of Paris

Pont Neuf

Pont Alexandre Iii

Pont Alexandre Iii

Canal Saint-Martin

Canal Saint-Martin

Montparnasse tower

Rue De Rivoli

Palais de Tokyo
« MÈRE »
« VOICI VOS FILS »
« QUI SE SONT »
« TANT BATTUS »
PEGUY

Place de la Concorde

Fountain Des Mers

Louis Vuitton Foundation

Place Des Vosges

Quartier Latin, Paris

Quartier Latin, Paris

La Petite Ceinture

Musée de la Vie Romantique

Galerie Vivienne

La Coulée Verte

La Coulée Verte

La Coulée Verte

Marché aux Puces de St-Oue

Shakespeare & Company Book Store

Acknowledgement

Page No. I Author/s I Title I Source I License

Shakespeare & Company book store	Ilkka Jukarainen	6Q3A71 07 (2)	https://www.flickr.com/photos/ 130333033@N08/4777643568 2/	Attribution-ShareAlike 2.0 Generic (CC BY-SA 2.0)
Rue de Rivoli	Anyul Rivas	Rue de Rivoli	https://www.flickr.com/photos/ anyulled/13124424164/	Attribution 2.0 Generic (CC BY 2.0)